Arlington
National Cemetery

Where Heroes Rest

Arlington
National Cemetery

Where Heroes Rest

Bob Temple

THE CHILD'S WORLD®, INC.

Library of Congress Cataloging-in-Publication Data
Temple, Bob.
Arlington National Cemetery : where heroes rest / by Bob Temple.
    p.   cm.
Includes index.
Summary: Introduces the history of our national burial ground and discusses some of
the people, particularly those in the American military services, who are buried there.
ISBN 1-56766-758-9 (lib. bdg. : alk paper)
1. Arlington National Cemetery (Arlington, Va.)—Juvenile literature.
2. Heroes—United States—Juvenile literature.
[1. Arlington National Cemetery (Arlington, Va.)]   I. Title.
F234.A7 T46   2000
975.5′295—dc21   99-057099

Credits

© Bruce Jackson/Gnass Photo Images: 9, 30
© Cameron Davidson/Tony Stone Images: 29
© Henley and Savage/Tony Stone Images: 2
© Hulton Getty: 10
© James P. Rowan: 19, 20, 24, 26
© John Sohlden/Visuals Unlimited: 6
© Lee Foster: 23
© Mark E. Gibson/Visuals Unlimited: 16
© Nick Gunderson/Tony Stone Images: cover
© William B. Folsom: 13, 15

On the cover...

Front cover: The names on these graves in Arlington National Cemetery are easy to read in the early morning sunshine.
Page 2: Arlington National Cemetery is peaceful on a fall day like this.

Table of Contents

America is a great place to live. Americans are free to choose where they live, where they work, what they own, how they worship, and more. Our many freedoms are a big part of what makes America such a great place. Over the years, however, there have been many threats to our freedoms.

Our **military** groups have had to fight in many, many battles to maintain the freedoms we enjoy today. Our soldiers have also fought many battles to help people in other countries. Unfortunately, when there is a war or conflict, people are injured and killed. Many of the Americans who have died in these battles are buried in Arlington National **Cemetery**.

⇐ **This is the grave of Audie Murphy. He received the most honors of any World War II hero.**

A Place for Heroes

Arlington National Cemetery is the most important burial ground in the country. At least one person from each American war or conflict is buried there.

The land on which the cemetery is located is in Arlington, Virginia. It is just across the Potomac River from Washington, D.C., the nation's **capital.** Thousands of Americans are buried in the cemetery, and all of them have served our country in a special way. Most of them are soldiers who were killed in battle. Some were soldiers who served in a war and died years later. Still others are important citizens, such as presidents, who served the country during their lives. In a few cases, other family members are buried there.

There are people from every state buried ⇒ in Arlington National Cemetery.

The first battle that had an impact on Arlington National Cemetery was a battle over the land itself. A man named Robert Howsing was the first person to own the land. He was given 6,000 acres by the governor of Virginia in 1669. Eventually, the land was purchased by John Parke Custis. His family built a home there called Arlington House. The house was later occupied by Mary Custis and her husband, Colonel Robert E. Lee.

During the Civil War, Colonel Lee was a leader in the Confederate Army, which fought for the South. The property was in the northern Union's territory, however, so the Lee family was forced to leave.

⇐ **This 1864 photo shows Union soldiers at Arlington House during the Civil War.**

In 1864, Private William Christman became the first person to be buried on the site. Later that year, more burials took place after it was declared an official military cemetery. The bodies of many soldiers who died in the Civil War could never be identified. They were called **Unknown Soldiers.** More than 2,000 unknowns from the Civil War were buried near Arlington House in a memorial in 1866.

In 1882, the Supreme Court ruled the Lee family was still the rightful owner of the property. But with so many graves already located on the property, the Lee family didn't want the land anymore. They sold it to the United States government for $150,000. The government quickly took control of large amounts of land next to the cemetery, making it larger.

This stone is part of the memorial to the Civil War. ⇒

"E Pluribus Unum" means "One out of many."

Burial of soldiers who died in conflicts with other countries began in 1892. In 1899, soldiers who died in the Spanish-American War became the first to be brought back to America for burial in Arlington National Cemetery. A memorial for the Spanish-American War was created in 1902.

The memorial to the Spanish-American War ⇒
stands tall among the graves.

Because Arlington National Cemetery honors the **patriots** who served our country, it is a very special place. It also attracts many visitors who want to honor the patriots buried there. Large crowds come to Arlington on special American holidays such as **Memorial Day** and the Fourth of July. In fact, a Memorial Amphitheater was built because of the large crowds that visit each Memorial Day. In 1915, President Woodrow Wilson laid the cornerstone for the amphitheater, which opened in 1920.

⇐ **These visitors are walking on the stage of the amphitheater.**

Unknown But Not Forgotten

One of the most special areas at Arlington National Cemetery is the Tomb of the Unknown Soldier. Originally, this tomb held the body of an Unknown Soldier from World War I. This Unknown Soldier was laid to rest there in front of the Memorial Amphitheater on **Armistice Day,** November 11, 1921.

In 1937, the tomb was placed under 24-hour guard. Even today, an armed guard watches over the tomb all day and all night. Three additional unknowns were buried in the tomb in the years since. One was from World War II, one was from the Korean War, and one was from the Vietnam War.

The large tomb reads "Here rests in honored ⇒ glory an American soldier known but to God."

Francis R. (Dick) Scobee
Commander
Washington
May 19, 1939

Michael J. Smith
Pilot
North Carolina
April 30, 1945

Ronald E. McNair
Mission Specialist
South Carolina
October 21, 1950

Ellison S. Onizuka
Mission Specialist
Hawaii
June 24, 1946

S. Christa McAuliffe
Payload Specialist
New Hampshire
September 2, 1948

Judith A. Resnik
Mission Specialist
Ohio
April 5, 1949

Gregory B. Jarvis
Payload Specialist
Michigan
August 24, 1944

IN GRATEFUL
AND LOVING TRIBUTE
TO THE BRAVE CREW
OF THE UNITED STATES
SPACE SHUTTLE CHALLENGER
28 JANUARY 1986

There are several other memorials on the grounds of Arlington National Cemetery. Besides the Tomb of the Unknown Soldier and the Memorial Amphitheater, there is the Tomb of the Unknown Dead of the Civil War. You can also see the Confederate Monument and the mast of the battleship USS *Maine.* There is also a monument to those who died when the space shuttle *Challenger* exploded in 1986.

⇐ **The members of the *Challenger* crew have their faces carved on the memorial.**

Another special memorial is the one for President John F. Kennedy. He was **assassinated** in 1963, and his body was laid to rest in a special memorial near Arlington House. As part of the memorial, an "eternal flame" was lit, which burns 24 hours a day, seven days a week. Two of President Kennedy's children were also buried there. His wife, Jacqueline, was buried there following her death in 1994. And President Kennedy's brother, Robert F. Kennedy, was buried nearby after he was assassinated in 1968.

The eternal flame at President Kennedy's ⇒ gravesite glows bright even on sunny days.

F R (DICK)
SCOBEE
COMMANDER
SPACE SHUTTLE
CHALLENGER
LT COL
U S AIR FORCE
MAY 19 1939
JANUARY 28 1986

William Howard Taft is the only president other than John F. Kennedy to be buried at Arlington National Cemetery. However, many other important people are buried there:

★ Two of the astronauts killed when the space shuttle *Challenger* exploded are buried in the cemetery—Commander Francis Dick Scobee and Navy test pilot Michael Smith.

★ Two of the three astronauts who died in a fire on the launch pad for the *Apollo I* space mission were buried in Arlington in 1967.

★ Frank Irwin, one of the few Americans ever to walk on the moon, is buried in the cemetery.

⇐ **This is the grave of *Challenger's* commander, Dick Scobee.**

★ Pierre L'Enfant, the man who designed the city of Washington, D.C., is buried in front of Arlington House.

★ Robert Todd Lincoln, son of President Abraham Lincoln, is buried in a plot that overlooks the Lincoln Memorial.

★ General John "Black Jack" Pershing and Audie Murphy, two important figures in world wars, are both buried in the cemetery.

Perhaps the most amazing sight at Arlington National Cemetery, however, is the rows and rows of white gravestones that seem to go on forever. The cemetery is the final resting place of more than 220,000 Americans.

⇐ **The rows and rows of graves at the cemetery are an impressive sight.**

Memorial Day is a special day at Arlington National Cemetery. Memorial Day was declared a national holiday in 1888. On this day we remember the people who have died while serving our country. Because Arlington National Cemetery holds the gravesites of many of these people, special ceremonies are held there every Memorial Day.

The Old Guard—the troops that help guard the Tomb of the Unknown Soldier—places a small flag on every grave in the cemetery before dawn each Memorial Day. The flags remain on the gravesites until after the Memorial Day service ends.

This soldier is helping to put flags on all ⇒ of the gravestones on Memorial Day.

There are many people who have served our country in wars and battles around the world. Many of these people are still alive today. About 15 people are buried in Arlington National Cemetery each day. It is expected that the cemetery will be full by the year 2020. At that time, more than 250,000 people will have been buried there.

Many tourists visit Arlington National Cemetery each day. They tour the grounds, visit the monuments and memorials, and remember the many people who have helped to make America the great country it is today.

Glossary

Armistice Day (AR–mih–stiss DAY)
The holiday that marks the end of World War I is Armistice Day. The Unknown Soldier from World War I was buried at Arlington National Cemetery on Armistice Day in 1921.

assassinated (uh–SASS–ih–nay–ted)
When an important person is killed by another person, we say he or she was assassinated. President John F. Kennedy and his brother Robert F. Kennedy were assassinated. They are buried in Arlington National Cemetery.

capital (KA–pih–tull)
The city in which the government offices are located is the capital. Arlington National Cemetery is located across the Potomac River from our nation's capital, Washington, D.C.

cemetery (SEH–meh–tayr–ee)
A plot of land in which people are buried is called a cemetery. Arlington National Cemetery is the most famous cemetery in the United States.

Memorial Day (meh–MOR–ee–yull DAY)
Memorial Day is a holiday in which we remember those who died while serving America. Memorial Day is a special day at Arlington National Cemetery.

military (MIL–ih–tar–ee)
The military is the group of soldiers who fight to protect a country. Thousands of military soldiers are buried at Arlington National Cemetery.

patriots (PAY–tree–uts)
A person who loves his or her country and works to protect or support it is a patriot. People who serve America are considered patriots.

Unknown Soldiers (UN–nohn SOHL–jerz)
Soldiers who died in battle but could not be identified are called Unknown Soldiers. Arlington National Cemetery has several memorials that honor Unknown Soldiers.

Index

Web Sites

Learn more about Arlington National Cemetery:

http://www.arlingtoncemetery.com

http://tqd.advanced.org/2901/

http://www.mdw.army./mil/cemetery.htm

CRASH! Roger hit a park bench and flew over his bike into a pond. But Pongo and Perdy were together at last. Roger would have been furious with Pongo if he hadn't met Perdy's lovely human, Anita.

In time both couples were married and settled down to a very nice life. Roger worked on his latest video game ideas. Anita worked as a fashion designer. And they were all looked after with loving kindness by Anita's childhood nurse, Nanny.

The only dark spot on the horizon was Anita's boss,

Cruella De Vil!

Cruella owned the very exclusive House of De Vil. She designed and made beautiful clothes. And

she was simply MAD about FUR.

Oh, how she loved a spotted design Anita had drawn, inspired by Perdy's spotted coat. Cruella reworked the drawing to show a full-length coat made out of Dalmatian fur. It was a whole new look— and Cruella had to have it!

So when Cruella learned that Perdy and Pongo were the proud parents of fifteen puppies, she paid a visit to Roger and Anita. "Where are the puppies?" she demanded. "Put them in a bag. I'll take them with me now."

"They have to be with their mother for several weeks," Anita explained. "Fine," said Cruella, whipping out her checkbook, "then put them on reserve for me. How much would you like?"

"They're not for sale!" Roger told her through clenched teeth. But Cruella was not one to take no for an answer.

When Anita, Roger, Perdy, and Pongo went out for their nightly walk, Cruella sent her two hired hands, Jasper and Horace, to

STEAL the PUPPIES!

She just had to have that coat! They burst through the door, shoved Nanny in a closet, and locked it tight. Then they threw the puppies into a burlap bag.

The puppies squirmed and cried and whimpered, but it was no use. Long before Perdy and Pongo returned, the puppies were on their way to Cruella's mansion in the country.

Luckily for the heartbroken Perdy and Pongo, Horace and Jasper stopped at a pub to have a little drink. Sleeping on the doorstep of the pub was a dog named Kipper. Curious by nature, Kipper wondered why he heard puppies whimpering in the back of Jasper's truck. Getting the full story from Wizzer, the bravest puppy, Kipper followed the truck when it left the pub.

Back in London, Pongo and Perdy were very, very sad. Pongo decided to do the only thing he thought might help him find his missing puppies.

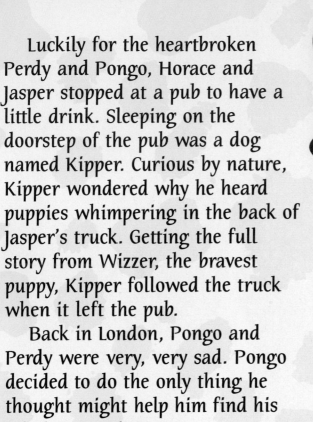

He climbed on the roof and began to BARK.

Pongo cried out into the night with **two** SHORT **barks,** one **LONG** bark, one SHORT bark, and a **howl.**

Suddenly, a Bernese mountain dog took up the cry. Then a Scottie chimed in. The message carried to a Welsh corgi guarding Buckingham Palace. He barked the message to a mutt in an alley who passed it to a mongrel on a barge.

Barking went on all night long across the countryside, all the way to a farmyard. There, a horse, cows, pigs, chickens, squirrels, rabbits, and a sheepdog named Fogey listened to Pongo's desperate story. When Kipper made his way to that very barn to ask for help, everyone volunteered.

Outside the barn, Fogey began to howl, sending a message back to London to Perdy and Pongo. They perked up their ears and scrambled to their feet, charging from the house. The two Dalmatians followed the code all through the night.

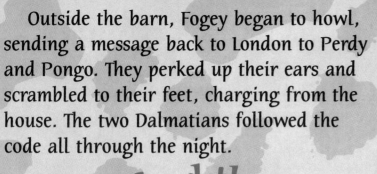

Would it lead them to their **missing puppies?**

Knowing that Pongo and Perdy had been alerted, Kipper went to the De Vil mansion. He jumped through a broken window and, nose to the ground, sniffed his way down the hall. In the mansion's library he found not one, not two, not even fifteen puppies, but thirty, forty, fifty— WHOA! He found ninety-nine Dalmatians!

Kipper had to think fast. There were ninety-nine puppies to sneak past Horace and Jasper!

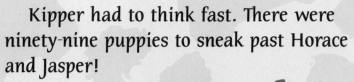

Rat-a-Tat-tAt

came a knock at the door. Jasper and Horace raced to answer it. Funny, no one was there. Kipper knew it was time for the ninety-nine Dalmatian puppies to begin their escape.

Rat-a-Tat-tAt

Puzzled, Jasper and Horace checked the door again, never noticing the little woodpecker who suddenly flew away! Jasper slammed the door shut. Poor Kipper needed more help!

TOOT! TOOT!

Playing with the horn of Jasper's truck, some raccoons got Jasper and Horace out of the house. Whew! That gave Kipper more time to move the puppies.

Even after outsmarting Horace and Jasper, and getting the puppies safely to the mansion's roof, Kipper wondered what he would do with them all. Thank goodness for Fogey! There was the sheepdog, down in the snow, catching Dalmatian puppies as they slid down a gutter to the ground below. But could they get away? They still had Jasper and Horace to deal with, and there was Cruella. Soon she would be hot on the puppies' trail!

No sooner did Kipper reunite the puppies with Pongo and Perdy at the farmyard, than Cruella found them! She pulled open the barn door, calling, "Puppies? Little sweetie puppy dogs? I'm not going to hurt you."

A smile spread across her gloating face. Soon she would have the puppies in her evil grasp!

SPLAT!

A host of cackling chickens in the rafters dropped eggs on Cruella's head! But even covered in yolk, she refused to give up.

"I know you're in here!" she said as a dangling tail caught her eye. Cruella reached up to the hayloft and pulled with both hands.

"I got you!"

Cruella yanked with all her might.

THUD!

A huge pig fell out of the loft, landing on Cruella. The pig let her up just in time to see Pongo and Perdy shepherding the puppies to safety!

Cruella's caper was over. The police arrived with Jasper and Horace, who had already turned themselves in. They escorted a snarling Cruella into the paddy wagon. She and her evil helpers would go to jail for a very long time!

What about the puppies? They moved out to the country with Anita, Roger, Nanny, Perdy and Pongo. And the family of 101 Dalmatians grew in size when those ninety-nine puppies grew up and had puppies...and their puppies had puppies...and their puppies had puppies...

The End

THE NATURE LIBRARY

HORSES

JAMES KERSWELL

CRESCENT BOOKS
NEW YORK

This 1991 edition published by Crescent Books,
distributed by Outlet Book Company, Inc.,
a Random House Company, 225 Park Avenue South,
New York, New York 10003.

Printed and bound in Hong Kong

ISBN 0-517-05154-0
8 7 6 5 4 3 2 1

Library of Congress Cataloging-in-Publication Data
Horses
    p. cm – (Nature Library)
    Includes index.
    Summary: Explores all aspects of the world of horses, including the range
of breeds and roles and practical information on selecting and caring for a
horse or pony as a pet.
    ISBN 0-517-05154-0 : $6.99
    1. Horses – Juvenile literature.   (1. Horses.)   I. Series.
SF302.H69 1991   90-41153
636.1 – dc20   CIP
                                                                    AC

The Author

James Kerswell grew up surrounded by horses and began his working
career as a groom at a stud and livery stables. His experience encompasses
not only the specialized care and exercise of quality thoroughbreds, but also
a great love of riding, mostly cross-country. He is currently employed in
forestry near the English/Welsh borders, where he also finds time to teach
at his local further education center.

Credits

Edited and designed: Ideas into Print, Vera Rogers and Stuart Watkinson
Layouts: Stonecastle Graphics Ltd. **Editorial assistance:** Joanne King
Picture Editors: Annette Lerner, John Kaprielian
Photographs: Photo Researchers Inc., New York, and Bob Langrish
Commissioning Editor: Andrew Preston
Production: Ruth Arthur, Sally Connolly, David Proffit, Andrew Whitelaw
Director of Production: Gerald Hughes
Director of Publishing: David Gibbon
Typesetting: SX Composing Ltd.
Color separations: Scantrans Pte. Ltd., Singapore

CONTENTS

Above: Horses are superb show animals and grace arenas around the world with their stately elegance and proud manner. This show in Bavaria is typical of many that draw vast crowds to admire both the skills of the riders and the discipline of the horses.

Left: A dwarf pony. Small ponies and miniature horses are ideal as mounts for children, although some small breeds are simply too tiny to be ridden at all. Many of the dwarf ponies are sturdy breeds well suited to the harsh environments in which they live.

ANCESTORS OF THE HORSE

The first known ancestor of the horse probably lived over 40 million years ago, before man evolved. Fossilized bones of the *Hyracotherium* (or *Eohippus*), found in the southern states of America, indicate a small creature, no more than 30cm(12in) tall, with four toes on the forefeet and three on the hindfeet. Over the next 15 million years it was to evolve into the bigger *Mesohippus* and *Miohippus*, animals with better teeth, suited to munching plants and foliage, and three toes on the forefeet, the central one being larger and able to carry more weight. By about 7 million years ago, *Pliohippus*, as it had become, was recognizable as the first fully-hooved type of horse, standing on what had been the central toe, the others having become non-functional.

By the time man appeared, this creature had evolved into *Equus*, the forefather of the three distinct types of horse that are adapted to different climatic conditions: the Steppe, the Forest and the Plateau. These are the ancestors of all today's horses. The Steppe type can be seen today, virtually unchanged, in Przewalski's horse (discovered by Colonel Przewalski in 1881), in zoos, and in the wild on the western edges of the Gobi Desert. The Forest horse, a much heavier breed than the Steppe, is now extinct, but is responsible for today's heavy coldbloods. The Plateau type was probably the ancestor of our finer-boned horses.

Below: Fossilized and skeletal remains of the earliest horse types are clues to the evolution of the modern animal. They reveal changes in face and body shape.

Left: The Islamic conquerors took a large, finely built and sure-footed Barb horse with them to southwest Europe. Originally an ancient desert mountain breed from northwest Africa, crossed with Arabs, further breeding resulted in the strong but intelligent Andalusian. Many famous western breeds, including the Lippizaner and Knabstrup, are descended from this horse.

Left: Przewalski's horse is a stocky, strong-looking animal, also known as the Mongolian, or Asiatic, wild horse. Because of man's need to take over more and more wild but fertile land for agriculture and building, it has been pushed into a near barren environment where, surprisingly, it survives quite well.

Below: This very early form of a horse's skull is clear evidence that it has hardly changed its characteristics at all. Although body and skull sizes vary, they all have the same functions as are seen in the modern horse.

Above: Przewalski's horse has an unusual dark stripe down the spine, and zebralike leg markings. Overall it is dun coloured, with a lighter cream under its belly. The mane is wiry and the ears long and pointed like a mule's.

Right: The Forest Tarpan that still runs semi-wild in parts of Poland may have the zebralike stripes on its legs and the line down the back indicative of primitive types. It also has a very thick mane and long tail.

Above: *Mesohippus* is believed to have been the first form of horse to have started carrying its weight on the central toe, which was larger than the other two.

THE HORSE IN HISTORY

From the earliest times, man appreciated the value and usefulness of a large four-legged animal that could be tamed and trained. As a result, the strength, speed and intelligence of this versatile beast have been put to use in a great many different ways over the centuries. On land or battlefield, the horse has reshaped our lives and changed the course of history. Pulling the plough and the cart or turning the wheel, horses revolutionized life for their owners and prepared the way for the development of the engine and mechanization. The horse made us more mobile and allowed us to travel greater distances at speed, improving trade and communications.

The horse provided various modes of transport. For example, a single rider could cover great distances at a good speed by changing horses at planned stopovers. Horses pulled carts and carriages, providing greater comfort and the opportunity to transport heavy goods and materials. We still measure the size of a motor engine in comparative horsepower

The horse's natural speed and grace have provided sport and entertainment for many centuries. The Ancient Romans enjoyed horse and chariot racing, and every culture has a traditional horse-based sport, from Spain's bullfighting to Tibetan and Japanese horseback archery competitions.

Right: This fine statue of a Przewalski's horse was found in the tomb of Emperor Qin Shihuang. The fact that it was buried alongside the emperor is evidence of the high esteem in which it was held.

The horse's role in battle has, perhaps, been the most important. Until the industrial revolution, and the rapid development of tanks, jeeps and aeroplanes, the cavalry was a crucial sector of any army. Special breeds of horses, such as the strong Salerno, were developed specifically for use in battle. The Australian Waler was still in great demand during the First World War, as a remount and artillery horse for the Allied troops in Europe, the Middle East, India and Africa.

Above: A primitive Egyptian tomb engraving shows that horses were ridden at that time.

Left: This cave drawing of a horse, found in the Cave of Niaux in France, indicates man's early interest in the animal.

Right: A proud, elegant-looking horse is pictured among a wide range of other animals. They are all part of the Roman mosaic at the ruins of Volubilis.

Above: Yabusame, the Japanese mounted spectacle, originates from ancient fighting techniques, which involved firing a bow on the gallop.

Below: From these Anasazi Indian cave paintings in Arizona, we can see that horses were ridden in posse, in a very similar style to the way they are today.

Above: Figures have been cut into the English chalk downs throughout history and the horse was always a popular subject.

Below: Jousting was once a serious test of a knight's skills. It is still performed today, but is regarded as a 'fun' event.

THE ANATOMY OF THE HORSE

Although all horses have the same basic anatomy, they can vary enormously in size, shape and colouring. The head or neck may be much longer, or the back and stomach more rounded; the legs can be short and stocky or long and slender; the coat sleek and glossy or rough and hairy. Such diversity is due either to the breed adapting naturally to certain climatic conditions, or to deliberate cross-breeding by man to produce a horse to suit his particular needs. From the big, muscular, heavy draft horses, such as the Rhinelands or Percherons, to the tiny Shetland ponies, all have been developed or bred to a purpose. It can be difficult to guess the origins of many closely bred horses, because they seem so perfectly developed for a particular role. Being so adaptable, a great many types have been developed in a remarkably short time.

Long, slim-legged breeds are best for speed; stocky cob types make a good all-round working horse. The finer, more spirited breeds are chosen for showing and jumping. The hairier breeds probably originated in a cold climate or lead mostly outdoor lives. Although hearing and eyesight are similar in all breeds, in the wilder horses these faculties may be more finely developed, especially among stallions, which are constantly on the lookout for predators or rivals.

Horses serve as beasts of burden, as a means of

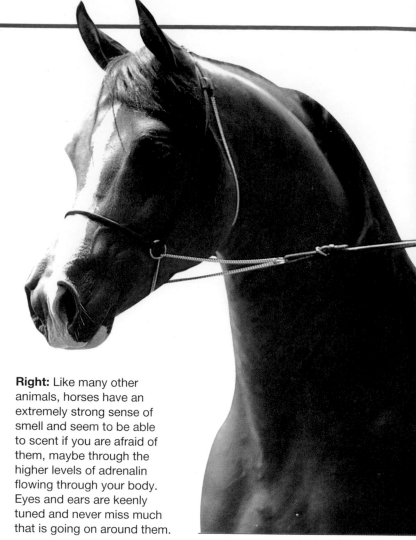

Right: Like many other animals, horses have an extremely strong sense of smell and seem to be able to scent if you are afraid of them, maybe through the higher levels of adrenalin flowing through your body. Eyes and ears are keenly tuned and never miss much that is going on around them.

transport or a source of power for pulling and pushing. It is quite amazing how tough and resilient a horse's body can be – and it will be pushed to the limits of stamina and speed for both work and sport.

Left: Small as they are, these two delightful Shetland ponies have the same characteristics as any of the other, larger breeds of horses in the world.

Above: The magnificent Percheron is a huge breed, famed for its power and muscle and valued for its ability to pull and shunt heavy loads around.

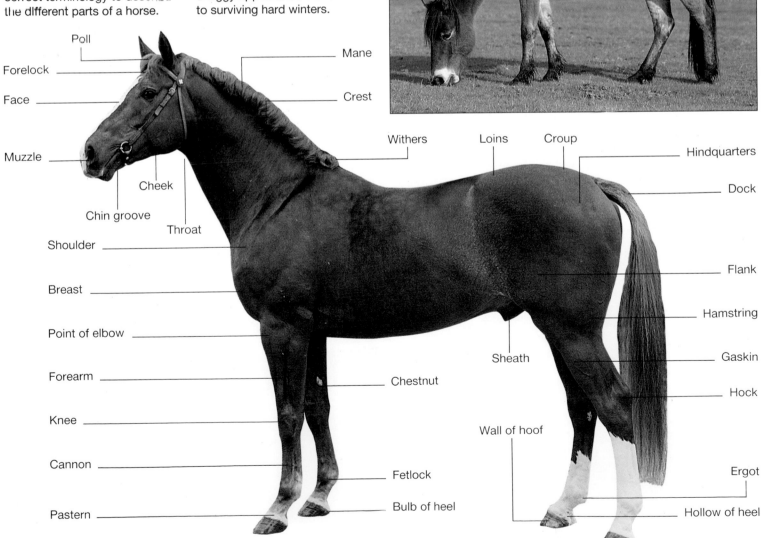

Above: The Saddlebred horse originates from the United States. It is very nimble and graceful, and displays its elegant physique in all its movements.

Below: You will find it useful to learn at an early stage the correct terminology to describe the different parts of a horse.

Above right: The strong Cob is capable of carrying a heavy rider thanks to its stocky body and well-set, sturdy legs. It usually has a gentle nature.

Right: The wild moorland pony is lean but compact, with a shaggy appearance well suited to surviving hard winters.

Poll
Forelock
Face
Mane
Crest
Muzzle
Cheek
Chin groove
Throat
Shoulder
Breast
Point of elbow
Forearm
Knee
Cannon
Pastern
Withers
Loins
Croup
Hindquarters
Dock
Flank
Hamstring
Sheath
Gaskin
Hock
Chestnut
Wall of hoof
Fetlock
Ergot
Bulb of heel
Hollow of heel

FUN FOR ALL THE FAMILY

Horses and ponies are hard and useful workers, but they are also enjoyed for sport and leisure all over the world. If you own a horse of your own, there are a great many activities and events you can enjoy together at weekends and in your spare time – depending on the type of horse or pony you have. You would not use a Shetland pony for show jumping, for example. If you would like to participate in a particular sport or activity, you should consider what kind of horse would be the most suitable, before you buy.

It is never too soon to start riding, and Pony Clubs hold classes throughout the year for the youngest, most inexperienced riders. These aim to help them to learn – or improve on – their riding and jumping techniques, as well as how to care for their horse.

For older riders there are more advanced courses, and riding or trekking holidays on which you may take your own horse or hire one are becoming increasingly popular. Wherever you live, there will be a wide range of horse-based events throughout the year.

Point-to-point events (cross-country) are fun for all the family. A set route is followed across country, giving horse and rider the chance to tackle a wide variety of different obstacles. Gymkhanas are a good opportunity for children and their ponies to display more formal jumping and riding skills in games and competitions. Keen competitors can win cups and rosettes. Both horse and rider should be well groomed for such events; indeed, grooming and preparation are

Left: When you have learnt how to handle your pony or horse with confidence, you can begin to attempt more advanced riding techniques, such as jumping small fences and obstacles.

all part of the fun of the day. Treasure hunts and rallies are designed for all ages - a more informal combination of good riding exercise with an enjoyable social event for both horse and rider.

Left: There are many pony clubs around the country. They organize regular gymkhanas, where youngsters can meet fellow riders and compete for rosettes. These fun events are also a good chance to observe, learn and improve on new skills and take up new challenges.

Right: Some horses are good-natured enough to tolerate almost anything and may even allow themselves to be dressed up to compete for the first prize in the local gymkhana fancy dress class. Most appear to enjoy the event as much as their riders, wearing funny hats and frills with apparent unconcern.

Left: Mounted games require a good deal of practice. Success relies on a good relationship between horse and rider for single-handed cornering.

Right: A horse needs to be manoeuvred in a natural manner to win prizes at eventing. This is especially important while judging is taking place.

Below: Trekking holidays are enormous fun for keen riders, especially when the whole family can explore new and unfamiliar countryside. Expert supervision is essential for maximum safety.

Below: For the more serious and experienced riders, cross-country events represent a test of both stamina and skill.

Below: On a fine day, hacking can be a very pleasurable activity, particularly if you have access to open countryside.

SPORT AND SPEED

In addition to the horse or pony that a family would keep at home for general riding and leisure purposes, some horses are specifically bred for certain activities and sporting events. They generally need extra care and attention and can cost a considerable amount of money to buy and insure.

Racehorses, or thoroughbreds, are used for flat racing or steeplechasing (racing over fences and hurdles) and, for the safety of both horse and rider, should only be ridden by a skilled and experienced jockey. Such sporting events are dangerous and a fall can result in serious injury. Apart from traditional racing, there are a wide range of other sophisticated sports involving riding and driving horses.

Skijoring (racing on ice) requires both skill and nerve. The horse has no rider; instead, the competitor is towed behind on skis, using two traces attached to the harness, and steered by two long reins. This sport can be extremely dangerous, sometimes even fatal, if one competitor becomes entangled in the traces of another's horse and is dragged under the hoofs.

The US and Canada are famous for rodeos – one of the best known being the Calgary Stampede, where a wide range of events and games are held, mostly involving horses. One of the most spectacular is chuck wagon racing, where a team of four horses draws the traditional mobile ranch kitchen around at a fast and furious speed. Equally exciting is campdrafting – where horses are used to catch young bullocks.

Other horse-based sports can be team games; a horse-mounted form of basketball is popular in France. In the game of polo, a small ball is hit with wooden mallets, and this fast and exciting game is enjoyed in many countries throughout the world.

Below: Chuck wagon racing is a fast and furious event, involving a large number of horses, some mounted and others drawn around the arena. It is surprising that they do not all become entangled with one another in the ensuing hustle and bustle.

Left: The racehorse can be used in several different events, such as steeplechasing or flat racing. They must undergo a great deal of rigorous training and can cost their owner a fortune to acquire, depending on their pedigree and past form. Jockeys are usually small and light but fit and muscular.

Above: Skijoring is a sport that is enjoyed by many people in Switzerland. It takes place on a frozen ice track and is both dangerous and exciting for all the participants.

Above: Polo ponies are very agile and fast, as they need to be able to turn quickly and take a good deal of rough treatment from the other horses. The players have to be able to guide the reins single-handed when they manoeuvre the ball.

Above: Every country has its own version of a horse-mounted spectacular, often performed annually at a festival or similar event. For the Berber horsemen of Marrakesh, Morocco, it takes the form of an elaborate fantasy sequence, with horses and riders elaborately attired.

Right: The show-jumping horse needs to have very strong back legs to give it the power to clear both vertical and horizontal obstacles of considerable height and breadth. As well as this physical strength, the horse must have good timing if it is to clear a jump successfully.

A HORSE FOR YOU

When choosing your horse, it is most important to know exactly how you are going to care for it and for what purpose you will use it. You will need the time and facilities to look after it correctly, and must be prepared to groom it, feed it, clean it and muck it out regularly. You must have sufficient room to keep a horse: a good stable or shelter, and a field or paddock for it to run about in.

Having satisfied all these requirements, you should consider the type of riding you would like to do – although there are people who keep horses and ponies purely for the pleasure of owning them. In this case, you should make arrangements for someone to ride and exercise the animals regularly. The horse's size and build are important considerations; they should match the rider's own weight and requirements.

Ponies and small, good-tempered horses are ideal for young children. If you want a strong, good-natured horse that can carry plenty of weight, a cob is a natural choice. The small, dainty hack is considered a good mount for a lady, but if you intend to hunt, you will need a nimble, intelligent horse with plenty of stamina. The polo pony should be fast on its feet and quick to turn.

It is always best to seek the advice of a veterinarian before you buy or, at least, ask someone with sufficient experience to check the horse for health and condition. For example, it can be very difficult to tell the age of a horse beyond about nine years old. The best age of horse for an inexperienced rider is around eight years, when the horse should have been fully trained and be ready to ride.

Below: To own a horse is a wonderful thing, especially if you have formed a good relationship with it.

Above: Your veterinary surgeon should detect any signs of eye trouble at an early stage.

Above: Before buying a horse, make sure the feet and joints are checked for any likely problems.

Above: The legs and feet are also included in regular veterinary examinations.

Above: Standing upright, a horse is measured from the floor to its withers (shoulders).

Left: Horses are very lovable creatures; some owners enjoy scenting their horse's breath, and the horse also seems to find this a pleasurable experience.

Right: By stroking and quietly talking to your horse, it will get to know and trust you. In this way, you can slowly build up a long-term caring relationship.

Below: Children love a pony of their own to look after and the experience teaches them a useful sense of responsibility.

Below: The local riding stables can supply a suitable mount for people who cannot afford a horse or pony of their own or who do not have space to house one. Stables cater for all age groups and riding skills.

Below: Horse auctions are a good place to buy an animal and you may be able to pick up a bargain. However, it is essential to take someone with you who has experience of horses and who can give you expert advice.

Above: This man is 'running up' a horse to show to a prospective buyer or veterinary surgeon.

A HOME FOR YOUR HORSE

Wherever you keep your horse or pony, you must be sure that it is absolutely secure – an escaped horse is a nightmare and a liability both to itself and others. The situation is particularly dangerous if the animal escapes onto a main road or into a built-up area, where it will become frightened and be difficult to recapture. It will also be at great risk of injury from traffic.

Fences should be strong and well maintained. Avoid materials such as sheet metal or barbed wire, as a horse can be seriously - even fatally – injured by them. Timber is a good versatile material for both buildings and fencing, since it is easy to maintain and replace. Keep fields and paddocks tidy, with no rubbish, especially glass, on which the horse could injure itself. Some plants are poisonous and should be removed: yew, laburnum and the rampant ragwort are just some that must be removed or eradicated.

Stabling can be designed to shelter one or several horses, and could be as simple as a loosebox or more elaborately divided into separate stalls. Site windows well out of reach and fit secure bolts onto stable doors – to stop both mischievous children and clever horses from opening them.

Keep the stabling clean and store manure in a separate place to prevent infestation by flies and parasites. Plenty of good-quality bedding is essential for various reasons: it helps to prevent draughts, encourages the horse to urinate and protects the animal from injury when it gets up and lies down.

Above: Sometimes it is a good idea to keep young horses together in a stable, because they tend to get bored on their own and become restless. Later on, as they grow, they will need more space, and can occupy separate compartments within the same building or sheds.

Left: When you are taking your horse back into the clean stable, always take it right in through the door – and close the door behind you – before letting the horse go. If you do release the horse at the doorway, you run the risk that it will not go into the stable but, instead, will decide to turn and run off.

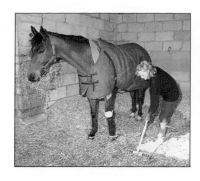

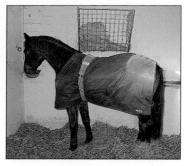

Above: Mucking out the stable is an everyday routine, usually performed every morning before breakfast. The dirty straw is removed and generally kept in one heap around the back or at the side of the building.

Below: In years gone by, this was a familiar sight in the countryside amongst the heavy working cart and farm horses. Each horse had its own individual cubicle where it could eat and rest; these were built on similar lines to cowsheds.

Above: Horses that are to take part in a show or special event are often 'rugged up' the night before. Covering them with a blanket prevents them from getting dirty and marked with unsightly wet stains overnight.

Right: If horses are kept in stables all the time, they tend to become bored and uneasy. It is much better – and more natural – for them to have somewhere where they can roam freely and gallop in the fresh air to let off steam and get some exercise.

Left: Once all the stables have been cleaned and fresh bedding has been put down, it is time to turn your attention to the outside. It is just as important to clean the surroundings on a regular basis, otherwise drains become clogged and the whole area will begin to look untidy.

Right: Some horses are easier to feed from outside the stable. It means you can avoid going inside, particularly if the animal has a nasty temperament. Haynets and water can be hung at a convenient height so that the horse can reach them from over the door or gate, without the risk of tangling.

ALL THAT TACK

Whatever type of horse you choose, you are going to need a certain amount of equipment – more, perhaps, than for any other animal or pet. Even the bare essentials can be fairly expensive, but there is a thriving secondhand market for such items, which can help the budget a little.

Equipment is necessary, not just for the horse but for the rider, too. Safety hats are vital in case of a fall, and are available in various shapes and sizes. Boots, gloves and jodhpurs can be improvised for everyday riding, but you need to be smart for special events, such as show jumping or eventing.

A horse that is taken to shows and events needs extra equipment: bandages, rugs and boots for protection and comfort during travelling, so that it arrives in top condition for judging.

Other items are simply essential in order to ride a horse. Bits vary a great deal, the most common being the snaffle, and even this is available in several different forms. Choice is usually a matter of personal preference. You will find a wide range of that most important piece of equipment – the saddle. Although expensive, it should last a long time if well maintained. Choose the saddle carefully, making sure it fits the horse and is comfortable for the rider.

There are a great many other necessary pieces of equipment: girths, bridles, numinals, martingales and

Above: The amount of tack available today is vast; this photograph illustrates just some of the principal pieces of equipment necessary for the good grooming and safe riding of any horse. Look out for good quality, secondhand items.

stirrups are all manufactured in different styles and sizes to suit every horse. Keep your tack well cleaned at all times to maximize its use. Leather should be saddle-soaped to keep it clean and supple.

Left: The lungeing cavesson is a useful piece of tack, particularly during training. It fits over the head and is similar to a bridle without the bit. A swivel and a long piece of rope or strong cord are attached to the front.

Above: The comfort of the bit you choose for your horse's mouth depends on the structure of the bars. If you use a bit that is twisted and sharp, it can cause pain and discomfort.

Right: Making the right choice of tack and equipment will ensure that both horse and rider are comfortable, safe and well prepared for whatever aspect of the sport they pursue.

Right: Certain horses, such as the indoor type and the neatly clipped racehorse, need to be kept warm when the weather is poor. A good-quality rug will help to retain body heat and prevent chills. Some rugs are also waterproofed, which is useful in winter and for taking the horse into and around the stable when it is cold and wet.

Above: Specially designed saddles to suit an owner's particular requirements can cost as much as the horse, because of the hours of labour involved.

Above: A double bridle has two bits: the snaffle bit, known as the bridoon, and the curb bit. Each one has an independent action, enabling the skilled and experienced rider to give the horse more precise instructions.

Right: This brown stallion is being led using the bridle as a head collar – a good idea, particularly if you do not have much time to spare for loosening up the horse's limbs using the lungeing cavesson.

FEEDING YOUR HORSE

Food and water are the two most important things in a horse's life. Without the right amount of food and a regular supply of water, the animal will grow thin, lose condition and die within a relatively short space of time. This is often seen in wild ponies and horses, particularly during a hard winter or in drought conditions. Sadly, horses can also suffer this kind of neglect at the hands of their owners, sometimes through ignorance, but often through lack of care.

A horse that does not work in any way does not require the same amount of food as one that works and exercises hard, and overfeeding can be as harmful as undernourishment. An overfed animal is easily recognized by its stomach bulging on either side, and its flabby muscle joints. This should not happen if your horse is fed the correct amount of food and given a moderate amount of exercise.

Some hay is very dusty, which can cause respiratory problems for your horse. You can avoid this risk by first soaking the hay in water. Horses need a lot of bulk feeds, such as greens, or dried foods, such as hay, alphalpha, silage, oat-straw and beet-pulp. These items enable them to digest more concentrated feeds, such as corn oil, oats, barley, beans, peas and linseed. Although both bulk feeds and concentrates contain plenty of the right vitamins and minerals, it is a good idea to provide extra supplements, in the form of feed blocks and licks, to ensure that the horse is receiving a balanced diet, particularly in areas with poor grazing and pasture with low nutrient levels.

Above: There is a wide variety of different foods that you can feed your horse or pony, but always take into account any particular dietary needs. Ensure that the diet includes an appropriate balance of proteins, minerals and carbohydrates.

Below: A horse's natural food is, of course, grass. If necessary, it can generally survive on pasture alone, provided that there is a sufficient supply of it, and that the grass contains an adequate level of nutrients. If necessary, offer a dietary supplement.

Above: It is essential that fresh drinking water is available at all times. Make sure the bowl or pail is kept clean to prevent disease.

Left: If hay contains harmful dust, douse it thoroughly with clean water in the haynet.

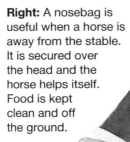

Right: A nosebag is useful when a horse is away from the stable. It is secured over the head and the horse helps itself. Food is kept clean and off the ground.

Above: Stabled horses need to be fed just the right amount of foodstuffs to keep them in peak condition. Hayracks, mangers and nets are all useful aids for ease of feeding.

Left: When the weather is cold and snow settles on the ground, it is hard for animals to find enough grass. Outdoor horses and ponies must be fed for as long as the bad weather lasts.

Below: Sometimes, it is only possible to attend to a horse once a day. In this case, it is important to provide extra hay or feed to last throughout the day.

GROOMING YOUR HORSE

Grooming your horse – giving its body a thorough clean and brush up – is important to keep it in good condition and free from parasites and disease. The lengths to which you might go in grooming activities depends on the type of horse you keep, although it is necessary to give any horse a good grooming once in a while. If you keep your horse purely for pleasure, such as weekend riding or occasional trekking, for example, and you don't have a lot of time to spare, then it is likely to spend a great deal of time wandering freely in a paddock getting fairly muddy. You should aim to give it a good clean at least once or twice a week, particularly around the saddle if it has been ridden and put in a sweat, to prevent saddle sores.

The initial grooming is done before the horse is let out, and this is usually known as quartering, quite simply because the body is divided into four areas and worked on in sequence. This routine clean and dust off should include picking out the feet, where sharp objects might lodge and cause a considerable amount of damage and discomfort. A stabled horse requires a lot more attention, particularly if it is a top-quality breed. So it is necessary to prepare and finish the basic procedures properly as follows. First use a dandy brush to clean off the dirt. Then use the body brush to remove grease, dried sweat and dust, cleaning it occasionally with a curry comb. Finally, a sponge and warm water will remove any stains on the coat.

Above: There are a number of stages in grooming a horse. The first is to clean the surface dirt off the body using a stiff-bristled brush, known as a dandy brush.

When a horse has been fetched in from exercise, the procedure is followed more thoroughly and is called strapping. This is not recommended for field horses since it removes essential oils from the skin, leaving it more exposed to the elements, although a quick wipe over with a dry cloth does not usually do any harm.

Left: A horse that is accustomed to being groomed will obligingly pick up its legs up when they are stroked and pushed backwards.

24

Above: In another grooming sequence, the body brush is swept over the horse's body and the curry comb is used to clean off loose hairs and dirt.

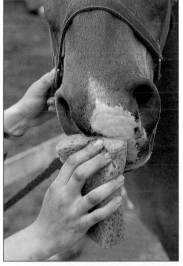

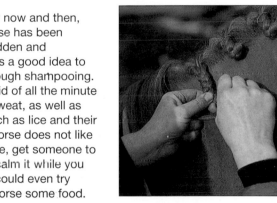

Right: Cleaning the legs can take quite a long time, because they are likely to be the dirtiest part. Groom them every time the horse has been ridden or worked to prevent a build up of dry mud and dirt.

Right: Sponging off the horse's nose will keep it clean of sweat and unwanted dirt. As the muzzle is very sensitive, do not use brushes for this purpose, because it might cause the animal to buck in protest. Always hold the horse's head while it is being cleaned to stop the animal turning around.

Left: The hoof pick is used for hooking out any stones or similar objects likely to cause damage to the tender part of the hoof. This is an important procedure for both stabled and outdoor horses, because if the hoof sustains a cut, it can easily become infected, causing unnecessary discomfort.

Left: To give the horse's feet a nice shine, you can apply a hoof-oil solution using a small paintbrush or even a piece of old cloth. There are several different types of oil available under various brand names and some have a colouring in them to give a long-lasting shiny look for eventing and shows.

Below: Every now and then, when the horse has been continually ridden and exercised, it is a good idea to give it a thorough shampooing. This will get rid of all the minute particles of sweat, as well as parasites, such as lice and their eggs. If the horse does not like this procedure, get someone to restrain and calm it while you work or you could even try offering the horse some food.

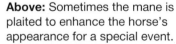

Above: Sometimes the mane is plaited to enhance the horse's appearance for a special event.

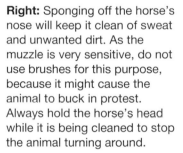

Above: The tail can also be plaited; it takes some time to acquire the knack of doing this.

EXERCISING YOUR HORSE

All horses require some kind of exercise. Leaving a horse alone in a paddock is not sufficient; it will quickly lose condition and become unfit. More vigorous exercise is necessary to help keep skin, bones and muscles well toned up, and lungs, heart and other internal organs functioning properly. Getting up a good sweat does a horse no harm at all; in fact, it is generally beneficial, as long as the horse is fit enough and is well wiped down and dried off afterwards. It is is a good way of exercising the glands and expelling unwanted salts and impurities through the skin, leaving the coat in a healthy and shiny condition. A horse should never be restabled in a sweat. It must be walked for a while to cool down, then dried with straw or some other suitable dry material to avoid chills.

Horses that are permanently stabled require more regular exercise than outdoor horses, because they do not get the opportunity to stretch their limbs and can become very unfit. There are ways of exercising a horse other than riding it. The lunge rein is a useful device, consisting of a set of reins about 6m(20ft) long, with a lungeing cavesson – a strong head collar that fits round the horse's head. The horse has no rider, but is encouraged to move around in a circular motion, controlled by the long reins. Every now and then it is made to move in the opposite direction.

Do not subject a fat, out-of-condition horse to long and stressful exercise, as this may put too much strain on the heart and muscles. A gradual exercise regime is recommended in this case.

Left: Jumping is equally good exercise for a horse. It is quite easy to provide facilities in the paddock or corral by placing just a few poles loosely across the top of some old oil drums.

Above left: When you arrive at a steep hill, it is far easier and more comfortable for the horse to canter along than to try to walk or trot up. The usual approach is for the rider to stand up in the stirrups and lean forward in the saddle.

Left: It is great fun to ride across the open countryside and feel the wind blowing in your hair and face. As long as the horse is not continuously driven hard, it will enjoy the exercise as much as the rider.

Left: Exercising a horse on the lunge rein takes quite a bit of practice before you are able to perfect the technique. Once the horse has been worked in one direction for a while, be sure to turn it, so that it exercises the other way round as well.

Above: Racehorses need to be exercised thoroughly every day of the week to prevent their muscles from becoming slack. They are usually trained in groups to encourage them to cope with race conditions.

Left: Horses that have not been led before may need encouragement. They can be attached to a carousel with several other horses, as shown here with these Quarter horses.

TRAINING YOUR HORSE

The majority of horses, except wild ones, of course, require some form of training, and this should start as early in life as possible. Training is important for the safety of the rider and for that of the horse itself. An untrained horse is a potential danger, especially if you intend to take it out on the road or public thoroughfare. You must be absolutely sure that it is not likely to buck, bolt or shy off into the middle of the road when faced with unfamiliar sights or sounds.

A young foal should have a head-slip fitted at the earliest opportunity, enabling you to lead it around and restrain it. A quick sharp smack on some solid part of the body, such as the neck, and a firm voice should be sufficient restraint, if repeated every time the animal misbehaves. Talking to your horse and stroking it as much as possible generally help to build up a confident relationship between owner and animal during early training. When the horse is about three years old, and used to being groomed and handled, it should be ready for riding.

There are several ways of training a horse to take a rider; some are not very kind and should be avoided, because the horse may lose confidence and develop bad habits. The best method simply requires time and patience. Accustom the horse gradually to the lunge-rein and to having a weight on its back. Use girth bands to accustom it to the saddle and fit a bridle long before anyone actually tries to mount the animal.

Above: When a horse has had a fair amount of training, it can start to practise jumping. To begin with, place small raised poles loosely over the top of two cross pieces of timber.

Below: If your horse has had no previous experience of jumping, you must approach this new challenge with caution. If the animal is at all frightened in the process it may injure itself. Begin by introducing, say, two or three poles laid on the ground and get the horse to walk over them. It will also help if you place a couple of upright posts at either end of the course to keep the horse working in a straight line.

Above: Once a horse has had plenty of practice at jumping over obstacles on its own with the lunge, you can consider introducing the saddle.

Below: Leading the horse or pony on long reins, and giving it commands as it is walked, will accustom it to obeying a variety of signals and controls.

Left: Do not take a horse onto the road until you are quite sure it can cope confidently. Consider the traffic around you carefully and signal for it to slow down; most drivers have the sense to do this automatically, so show your appreciation.

Right: You can begin training a young horse from a very early age. As soon as a newborn foal is able to run about alongside its mother, you can fit a head-slip, which will allow you to lead the horse about and control it if necessary. Remember to adjust the head-slip regularly, so that it does not become too tight as the head grows. At the same time, be sure to give your horse plenty of verbal encouragement and pats.

BREEDING YOUR HORSE

Breeding horses and ponies can be a long and complicated process. First you must find a suitable sire for your mare, or vice-versa. If you are hoping to breed top-quality show jumpers or racehorses, the cost can be quite considerable. You should be clear about the kind of animal you are hoping to produce. If you want to breed a certain type of foal, you must obviously make very careful plans, and the parents must be selected and matched with care.

Breed stallions usually have the mare brought to them, unlike their rugged ancestors in the wild. Rival stallions used to fight to prove their strength, ensuring that only the strongest and fittest would sire the mares in the herd and thus produce good strong foals the following season.

When a mare has conceived, she carries the foal for approximately 11 months. She usually foals down in the spring, when the young animal would stand the best chance of survival in the wild. After proper care and feeding during pregnancy, a mare should give birth quite easily and requires no additional assistance, unless she has been sired by a stallion considerably bigger than herself. The birth should not take long and usually happens at night – probably because of an inbred instinct to avoid being attacked by predators or hunters while the mare is still vulnerable.

If you hope to breed from your own mare, remember that she will not be able to do any strenuous work during pregnancy, nor will you be able to ride or jump her.

Right: As soon as the foal has learned to stand up on its own, it will instinctively know how to suckle from its mother.

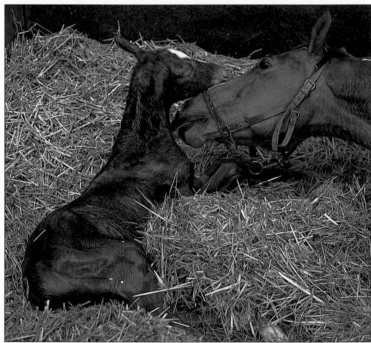

Left: Usually, the mare will give birth perfectly naturally and can tend to her foal's immediate needs. She will normally dispose of the caul (a protective membrane) by eating it and licking away at the amniotic fluid, but as a precaution you should quickly check that she has cleared the foal's head and nostrils so that it can breathe.

Above: Once the foal is dry and clean, the mother will be familiar with its scent. She will not allow any other horse to come near the youngster for several days.

Right: From the moment it is born, the foal's natural instinct is to make every effort to struggle to its feet and stand unaided, but it will be unsteady at first.

Left: The young horse is soon mobile and independent from its mother. However, it will not stray far from her in the early days.

Above: A mother will continue to give her foal every attention. Grooming is important and reassuring to the new arrival.

Right: Careful selection of a stallion for breeding plays an important role in the type and temperament of a foal, but it is not possible to guarantee the colour and eventual physical characteristics of the offspring.

CARING FOR A NEW FOAL

From the moment a new foal is born, you must make sure it receives adequate care and attention to prepare it for later life. The mother will provide most of its basic needs for some time – from the newborn foal's first feed of milk until the moment when it starts feeding itself on grass. The first feed, known as colostrum, is vital to the foal's survival, as it contains various antibodies, vitamins and nutrients. It does not resemble milk, but is a thick light green or yellow liquid. It is only after a few feeds that it starts to flow a purer, whiter colour. Should the mare be unable to suckle the foal for any reason, it is essential that you feed the young animal colostrum by hand.

As the foal grows older, it becomes less dependent on its mother for food, and starts to feed itself on grass and twigs. With their short necks and long gangly legs, the foals find this quite difficult at first, and they can be a comical sight as they try to reach the ground in all kinds of awkward postures.

Handle the foal as soon as possible, stroking and talking to it, so that it becomes accustomed to your presence. As time goes by, it should accept being handled more readily, and you will have established a confident relationship before any training starts. Separate the foal from the mare when it is five or six months old, but not before. It may show some distress for a day or so, but providing it is fit and healthy, it will soon be happily occupied in enjoying all the new experiences of a horse's life.

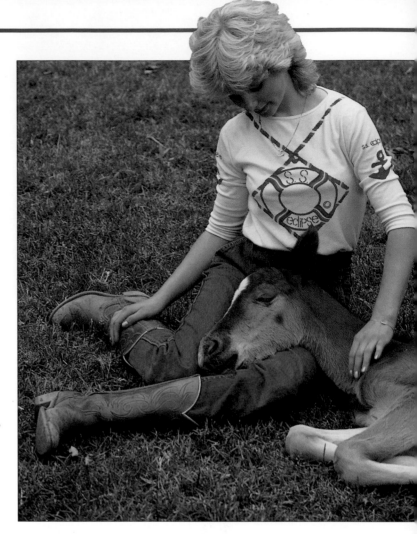

Above: There are several reasons why some foals may not get enough milk from their mother. Offer them additional feeds from a bottle and teat.

Right: This young Morgan colt is enjoying a turn around the paddock with its mother. They are better kept outside if the weather is fine enough.

Left: Getting to know a young foal is a pleasure and time well spent. It will encourage the horse not to be shy of you and to trust you when it gets older.

Right: The mother horse will continue to suckle the foal for some time. She will also take care of most of the grooming herself until the foal becomes more independent.

Below: From time to time, it is necessary to take either the foal or its mother into the stable. It is always a good idea to lead them in both together in order to avoid any unnecessary distress.

Left: As long as mother and foal are well looked after, they should remain content and healthy.

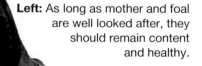

Below: Foals that are free to roam around in the field with their mother soon learn how to feed themselves on grass and foliage.

THE HEALTHY HORSE

Even with the best care and attention, a horse will become ill at some stage in its lifetime. Like all animals, it is prone to various diseases and viruses.

Most horses have worms and, unless they are treated at regular intervals, these can cause serious internal problems. The best method of treating them is by mouth, using a small drench-gun or simple syringe without a needle. Regular treatment should be part of your routine care for the animal and will prevent reinfestation.

Regulating your horse's diet will also help to avoid common problems. For example, putting your horse out to rich pasture when it has been used to poorer grass is a sure way to cause colic, and good grazing in the early summer may cause excessive weight gain. Regular grooming is equally important to keep the horse's coat and circulation in good condition.

Although this routine health care will do much to keep your horse fit and in good condition, there are a few regular tasks that a professional should carry out. You will need a farrier, or blacksmith, to attend to the horse's feet and shoes. Your veterinarian will check its teeth and vaccinate against two of the worst horse diseases: tetanus and influenza.

Above: A horse that is well cared for and given plenty of exercise will not only have a healthy outward appearance, but will also be able to move its muscles smoothly and easily.

It is useful to keep a record of such treatment, so that you know when your animal is due for its booster shots and as a guide should there be any adverse reaction to a particular treatment. If you add details of the cost of feed, tack and other necessities, you may also find the record useful for budgeting purposes.

Left: The teeth of a 28-year-old gelding. Note how they have slowly worn away so that they point forwards in the mouth.

Below: It is important to ensure that your horse's teeth are not wearing unevenly. Be sure to have them checked regularly by someone with experience.

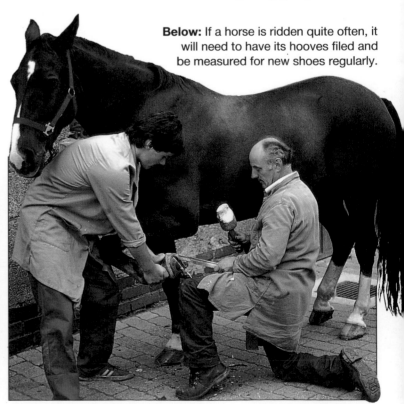

Below: If a horse is ridden quite often, it will need to have its hooves filed and be measured for new shoes regularly.

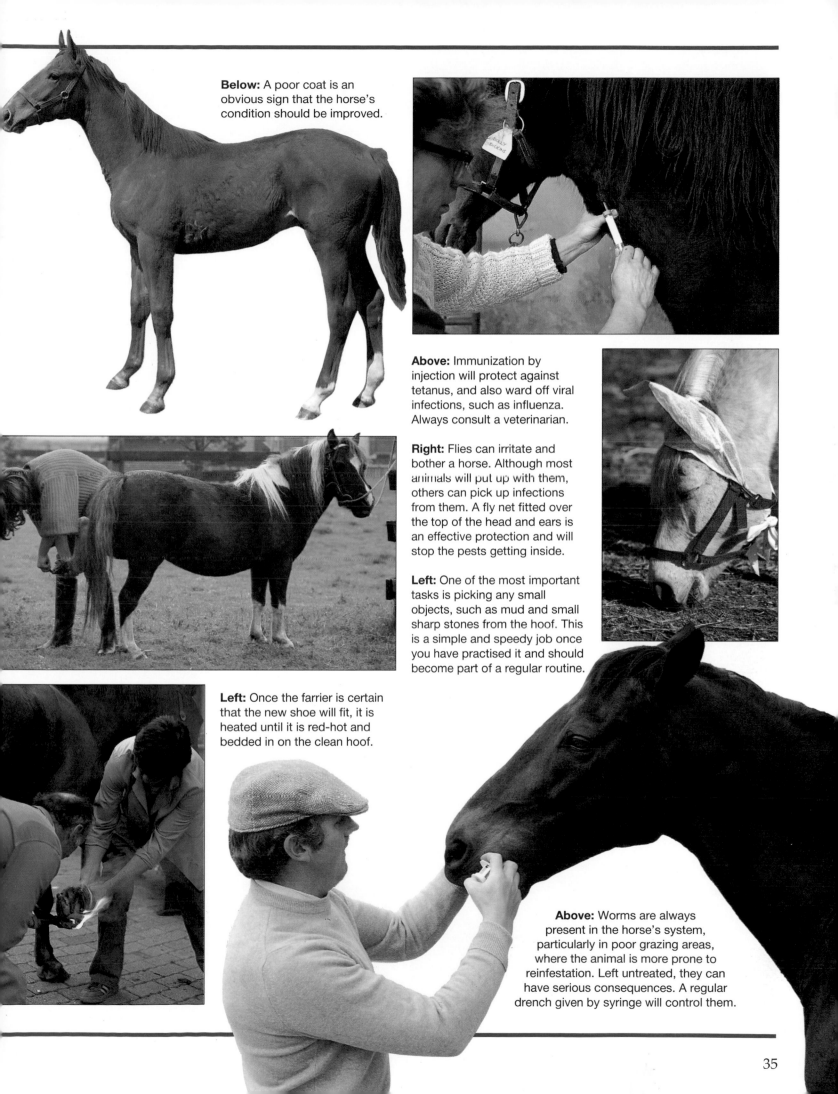

Below: A poor coat is an obvious sign that the horse's condition should be improved.

Above: Immunization by injection will protect against tetanus, and also ward off viral infections, such as influenza. Always consult a veterinarian.

Right: Flies can irritate and bother a horse. Although most animals will put up with them, others can pick up infections from them. A fly net fitted over the top of the head and ears is an effective protection and will stop the pests getting inside.

Left: One of the most important tasks is picking any small objects, such as mud and small sharp stones from the hoof. This is a simple and speedy job once you have practised it and should become part of a regular routine.

Left: Once the farrier is certain that the new shoe will fit, it is heated until it is red-hot and bedded in on the clean hoof.

Above: Worms are always present in the horse's system, particularly in poor grazing areas, where the animal is more prone to reinfestation. Left untreated, they can have serious consequences. A regular drench given by syringe will control them.

FIRST AID AND EMERGENCIES

As the owner of a horse or pony, you should be prepared for the possibility that the animal might suffer an injury or accident that could threaten its life or that demands immediate attention.

Many accidents can be avoided by eliminating dangerous objects from the paddock or stable. However, even the best cared-for horses do wound themselves sometimes and, unless attended to immediately, an abrasion can quickly become infected, requiring specialized treatment. This will be costly and time consuming, and will result in prolonged pain for the animal.

Keep any wounds as clean as possible but uncovered, so that the fresh air can help them to heal cleanly and quickly. A veterinarian should attend to lacerations, even if they are small. For bad bruising, continuous flushing with cold water is usually all that is necessary, and if there is a nearby stream, encourage the horse to stand in it at regular intervals.

A common problem is the puncturing of the horse's feet, allowing dirt and bacteria to enter the hoof and causing painful swelling. A poultice applied to the infected area should relieve the swelling and help to draw out the infection. Afterwards, you must keep the ground as clean as possible to prevent any germs re-entering the site of the wound.

Horses are also prone to skin problems, some of which can be passed on to humans, but by good stable management and regular grooming you should avoid the more serious infections. If your horse does become afflicted, antibiotic treatment is effective.

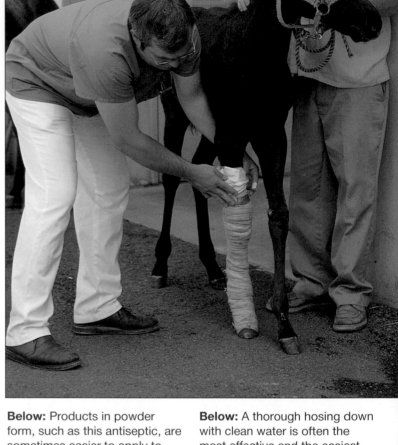

Below: Products in powder form, such as this antiseptic, are sometimes easier to apply to minor wounds and cuts on the legs than creams or lotions.

Below: A thorough hosing down with clean water is often the most effective and the easiest way to cleanse a potentially dirty wound around the hoofs.

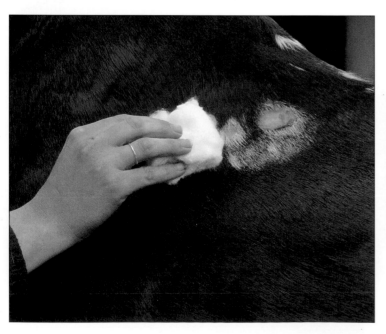

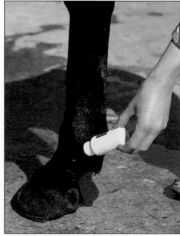

Left: Examine the horse for signs of saddle sores and apply prompt treatment at home with a proprietary lotion or liniment.

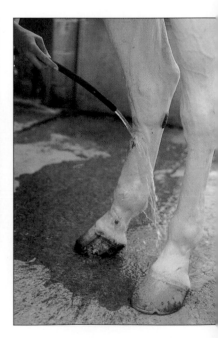

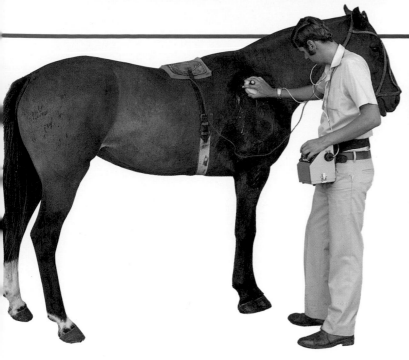

Left: Serious injuries may require treatment at the local veterinary centre or clinic. It is a good idea to accompany your horse, as this will help to calm it.

Above: Electric shock treatment is sometimes recommended for muscular strain, but should only be administered by an expert, so seek out qualified help.

Below: Maintain fencing in good condition. A horse could sustain a serious cut from a jagged edge, as well as escape.

Right: Depending on the severity of an injury, it may be necessary to inoculate the horse to prevent infection setting in.

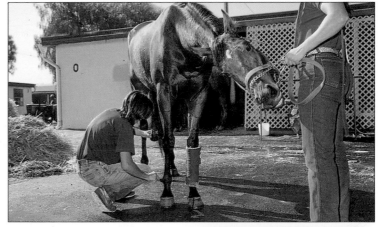

Above: Racehorses are highly bred and expensive to buy and keep. They require expert and conscientious attention at the slightest sign of trouble.

Right: Thoroughbreds receive the best possible treatment; here a horse is enjoying a whirlpool footbath, while the trainer offers it medication.

Left: Horses can sometimes hurt each other unintentionally, simply by being too boisterous when playing in the paddock.

TYPES AND TEMPERAMENTS

There are so many different types of horse that it is almost impossible to identify their origins. For generations, partbreeds have been mixed with purebreeds, and warmbloods with coldbloods, until the scope and variety is virtually endless. Usually, a particular horse will have been bred for a particular purpose, such as speed for a sporting horse, or a fine physique for showing.

The sporting types tend to be warmbloods – breeds with a fiery streak, making them sometimes temperamental but very agile and extremely fast; ideal characteristics in a racehorse or polo pony.

The heavier, bigger breeds do not usually have such a wild side to their character, which is maybe just as well – the idea of a carthorse taking off, galloping around, and jumping over obstacles is quite daunting. These more stolid horses are valued for their physical strength and dependability, making them good workers, able to pull a plough, barge, boat or dray. The powerful Hanoverians and Oldenburgers, have fine muscular bodies and well-controlled movements, making them perfect dressage horses.

Whatever type of horse interests you, it has probably already been crossed with several others to refine its strongest characteristics and make it better suited to a particular role. When choosing a horse for eventing, show jumping, dressage or simply as a family pet, intelligence and temperament are just as important as strength, grace and speed. All these factors can be influenced by careful cross-breeding.

Above: This fine Hanoverian stallion, with its strong muscular body, is famous as an athletic sports horse. Also known as the Isabella, it is perhaps Germany's best-known breed.

Left: The cob type of horse can usually be relied upon to be intelligent and have a tolerant temperament. Its strong stocky body is ideal for riding.

Right: These horses need to be high spirited and courageous to race against each other over the ice at great speed. This is a popular sport in Switzerland.

Above: Some horses remain little changed in appearance from thoir early ancestors; Przewalski's horse is a living example of how they looked.

Left: Sports are a good test of a horse's mood and intelligence, revealing just how it will react to unusual circumstances.

Above: The Shire horse is well known for its immense strength but, despite its size, it has a placid, friendly nature and is sometimes called the gentle giant of the horse world. Shires were once valued workhorses, but are seldom seen today.

Right: The Arab is a breed well known for its stamina, endurance, superb physique and good looks. As well as its physical attributes, it has an affectionate nature and is justifiably popular.

VARIATIONS IN DESIGN

Horses and ponies have a surprising variety of colours, from deepest black to pure white (albino), with reds, golds, browns and greys in between, and all kinds of markings – from spots and stripes to stars and speckles. Whatever the colour and pattern, a coat in good condition looks stunning and displays the colour to its best advantage.

Some horses combine several distinct shades. The striking Pinto, for example, might be black and white (called piebald) or brown and white (skewbald). There are several shades of brown – or bay as it is called – from dark bay to the reddish golden bay, and meal bay – a rusty colour. Chestnut horses come in various tones of reddish brown: dark chestnut, which can be nearly black; golden chestnut, with its hint of gold; and liver chestnut – supposedly the same shade as cooked liver.

Greys are often dappled, i.e. darker markings are shown against a light grey background; or flea-bitten grey, which is much nicer than it sounds – light grey speckled with reddish or brown hairs. Some colours are quite strictly defined. The Palomino – a colour specification, not a breed – is a stunning golden colour, with white tail and mane. Sometimes the legs have white markings, but there should be no other colours on the body.

Many horses have distinctive white markings: a wide mark down the whole of the face is called a blaze, while a narrower strip of white down the face is a stripe. The lovely splash of white on the forehead is called a star and white markings on the legs are socks.

Above: With its striking blond mane contrasted against a dark grey body, the South German Noriker is a handsome cold-blood that can trace its ancestry back to the Roman state of Noricum. It is a medium heavy horse, still found in mountain regions in Bavaria and Austria, where its adaptability and sure-footedness are valuable assets.

Left: Palomino is a distinctive colour classification for horses and ponies. It indicates that these very beautiful animals have a golden body with dark eyes and a white mane and tail.

Above: Lippizaners are the famous great white horses of Spain. Today, they are a speciality of the Spanish Riding School, Vienna, demonstrating their gymnastic ability.

Above: A Dun gelding. Various shades are all classified under the heading of Dun coloured, from the almost lemon-coloured Yellow Dun, to the mouse-coloured Blue Dun. All types have a black skin and muzzle.

Below: Chestnut-coloured horses come in several shades, from a bright golden to a colour resembling cooked liver. This chestnut has distinctive white stockings on the legs and a white blaze down the face.

Above: Contrasting spots on the coat are an attractive and immediately identifiable feature. These horses are a popular choice for children's ponies and are often featured as showy performing circus horses.

Left: Pinto is a North American term used to describe both the Piebald, with black-and-white markings, and the Skewbald, which is splashed with white and any other colour but black.

Below: The Paso Fino from Columbia is a compact South American riding horse, believed to have Berber and Arab blood. It comes in all colour variations and has an unusual gait.

PUREBREDS AND HALFBREDS

Today's thoroughbreds, or racehorses, can all be traced back to one of only three pure-blooded horses, from which they are all descended. These were, firstly, Byerley Turk, a horse captured and ridden in the Battle of the Boyne in Ireland by a Captain Byerley in 1690; secondly, the Darley Arabian, sent back to England in 1704 by Thomas Darley, then British consul in Aleppo (now in Syria); and, finally the Godolphin Arabian from the Bay of Tunis, presented as a gift to the King of France by Lord Godolphin in the 1730s.

Horses have been raced in various parts of the world for thousands of years. However, thoroughbreds, the fastest horses in world, were not developed as racehorses until the eighteenth century. They were bred mainly in England and, by the beginning of the twentieth century, these costly horses were the UK's fifth largest export.

Some horses are not noted for their fine breeding and have no specific pedigree but, as a mixture of several different valued breeds, they are ideally suited to a particular need or requirement. Certain horses are simply a blend of two distinct breeds and are known as halfbreds. The Anglo-Arab, for example, is half English Thoroughbred and half Arab. It was specially bred as an excellent lightweight saddle horse with a good nature, and is usually an elegant bay or chestnut colour. The Limousin Halfbred is a similar horse; originally a medieval French riding horse, it was crossed with Thoroughbreds and Arabs for hundreds of years, until it resembled as closely as possible the purebred Anglo-Arab. Other hybrids are the result of a horse crossed with some other closely related animal. For example, the mule is the offspring of a donkey stallion mated with a horse or pony mare to produce a tough hardworking animal known throughout the world; and the hinny is bred from a horse or pony stallion mated with a female donkey.

Left: Naturally strong and with good stamina, thoroughbreds were originally developed for their speed in hunting. However, it was not long before they were being raced, and foreign blood was introduced to strengthen the breed. Today, they are the fastest, most expensive horses.

Above: The hardy mule – half horse, half donkey – is a useful beast of burden, patiently carrying loads or pulling carts.

Above: The Italian Avelignese is a good hardy mountain pony with a quiet reliable nature. It looks very like the Austrian Haflinger, but is stockier and heavier and not as high spirited as this Arab crossbreed.

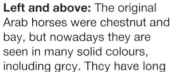

Left and above: The original Arab horses were chestnut and bay, but nowadays they are seen in many solid colours, including grey. They have long

been prized for crossing with other breeds to add elegance, spirit and intelligence, and these fine horses are also used for riding, showing and racing.

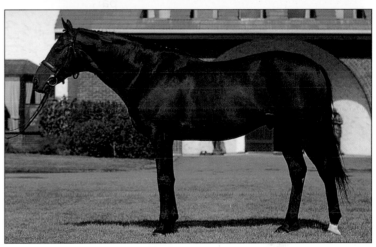

Above: Thoroughbred stallions are extremely valuable animals and it can be expensive to have a mare sired by one.

Above: The Anglo-Arab is half English Thoroughbred and half Arab - a kind-natured horse with a good-looking body, often grey.

Right: The purebred Arab was originally a desert horse. Speed, grace and a fiery temperament were its characteristic features.

SADDLE HORSES

The saddle horse is a good all-round riding horse, and every country has its own favourite, specially bred to provide a good-looking mount with a highly attractive movement, whether walking, trotting or cantering.

The classic fine saddle horse is the purebred Arab, which has contributed to the breeding of many half and mixed-breed riding horses. Within these specifications, types vary enormously, from the elegant but powerful French saddle horse and lightweight Hispano, to the tall sturdy Groningen, an ancient breed from Holland classed as a heavyweight saddle horse and also a good harness animal.

A great many of today's fine saddle horses were originally bred to produce the perfect cavalry horse, but are now valued as excellent riding or carriage breeds. Some, like the Hungarian Furioso, are outstanding in a great many roles, including show jumping, dressage, eventing and, in Eastern Europe, even in steeplechasing. One of the finest saddle horses is the American Saddlebred, or Kentucky Saddler, a handsome mixture of Thoroughbred and Morgan blood, with a touch of Narragansett Pacer – a now extinct riding horse with a lovely movement. This highly attractive horse is graceful as a dancer, and was originally bred as a showpiece for the rich.

Other good riding horses are better known for their toughness and endurance. The Jaf from Iran, for example, is equipped to survive the harsh conditions of mountain and desert, while the hardy Barb (native to Barbary, a region in North Africa) is an attractive, ex-cavalry favourite, capable of living in poor conditions.

Above: The gentle yet powerful Quarter horse is one of the most popular saddle mounts in the world and particularly in the US.

Left: The American Saddlebred, or Kentucky Saddler, is valued for its graceful movements. It is an excellent show and riding horse with a well-shaped head, fine physique and good nature.

Above: Popular as a French riding horse since medieval times, the Limousin has been further refined by breeding with thoroughbreds until now it is almost a pure breed itself.

Right: The Freiberger Saddle horse from western Switzerland is an intelligent and docile mount. Its strong stocky body and willing nature are well suited to its work in the mountains.

Above: Great speed, stamina and jumping ability have made the halfbred French Saddle horse a popular choice for competition riding, being widely used for show jumping, eventing and cross-country racing. It has the added advantage of looking as well as it performs, with an elegant yet powerful body and, although not a true purebred, it is a proud mix of Arab and French Trotter blood.

Below: The handsome Morgan is one of the most intelligent saddle and harness horses to have come out of America. It is a muscular and powerful mount, but easy to handle.

Below: Known as the great white horse of Spain, the Andalusian has been specially bred for centuries to develop its strong elegant body and quick responses.

SETTING A PACE

Some breeds of horses are particularly valued for their stamina and ability to set – and maintain – an elegant pace. For centuries, coach, trap and carriage drivers have taken advantage of this type of horse, either in great sporting events, such as chariot racing in Roman times, or for drawing wheeled vehicles, which are still used today in some parts of the world as the best means of transport. Elsewhere, the traditional carriage and trotting breeds are maintained for ceremonial purposes, competitions or displays, and for pleasure.

The Cleveland Bay, a good-looking strong horse standing at about 16 hands, is probably the oldest breed of carriage horse in the UK. A slightly smaller breed, the German Trotter, stands at about 15 hands and is very popular. This horse tows a small two-wheeled carriage, called a sulky, and is capable of pulling the vehicle for a surprising length of time.

Sulky driving is a favourite horse event in Germany, perhaps even more popular than thoroughbred racing, and several types of trotters are used for this particular style of racing. In France, the French Trotter is used for riding and driving. It is a much more powerful and taller horse than is generally seen in international trotting. All carriage or trotting horses used throughout the world have the talent to keep up a pace without losing any gracefulness.

Below: The American Standard-bred is extensively used for trot racing, a popular sport in the US that requires very fast horses.

Above: Racing at great speed is not only associated with good horsemanship, but is also seen as a test of driving skills. The horse is required to pull a light-weight buggy around a circuit carrying a single rider seated close behind the horse's legs.

Below: The Orlov trotters are a very common sight in Russia, where this sport is extremely popular. They are slightly slower than the American Standard-bred, but very striking, agile horses. They are generally grey, or maybe black or bay, and usually stand at about 15 hands.

Above: The French Trotter is a fine horse, although it has only been recognized as a breed for the last 70 years or so. It is only in France that riders continue to employ these animals in trotting races, as well as driven events. Some animals are also used for jumping, general riding and breeding. They are very strong, powerful horses, standing at around 16 hands high.

Right: These two American Standardbreds are battling against one another around the circuit in a bid to reach the finishing post. It takes great concentration on the riders' part to keep them going at a brisk pace, while preventing the horses from breaking into a full gallop. Leg straps are used to avoid this.

Left: One of the world's best carriage horses is the Friesian. It is a heavy, hard working and friendly breed, capable of working as one of a pair and easy for the rider to control. At one time it was much in demand for farmwork and transportation, but today its showy, high-knee trot often features in driving competitions, circus work and in historical re-enactments.

GIANTS OF THE HORSE WORLD

The massive coldbloods – the giant Shire and dray horses, standing up to 17 or 18 hands high – are a magnificent and awe-inspiring sight, especially when fully groomed and dressed in braids, bells, plumes and brasses for special displays and competitions. They are descended from the ancient Forest horse and were originally bred in the Middle Ages to bear the weight of a knight in full armour. This role became redundant when it was realized that a more lightly clad combatant on a smaller, more nimble horse was more effective in the heat of battle.

The heavy horse subsequently assumed a new and even more important function – for the last 500 years it has been a workhorse, an invaluable source of strength and power on the farm, in the forest or on the seashore. These gentle giants were bred even bigger and stronger for this purpose, yet their good nature and quiet intelligence are a welcome surprise in a beast so massive. They have never been completely superseded by the motor vehicle; teams of heavy horses are still used today in parts of North America, northern France and the UK, and where the terrain is not suited to a tractor or cart.

The UK has its Shire – the tallest horse in the world and a direct descendant of the old warhorse – and its powerful Suffolk Punch. France has bred the compact and lively Breton, the huge Ardennais and the strong but gentle Trait du Nord. Other countries have their own favourites: the Rhineland and Russian Heavy Draft horses, the Danish Jutland – another warhorse descendant – and Hungary's powerful Murakoz.

Above: Every country has its own breed of heavy horse and this sturdy Franches Montagnes still works on a Swiss farm in the Jura mountain region, where tractors are impractical.

Above: Lean but powerful, the Irish Draft horse can cope with the heaviest tasks. However, if it is crossed with a Thoroughbred, the result is an excellent eventer and good jumper.

Right: The Breton is not tall by heavy horse standards, but it is strongly built and muscular. It has a relatively square head, straight face and small ears and is often a red roan colour.

Above: This fine specimen, Jim's Chance, was champion Shire horse at an annual show.

Above: The white-faced Clydesdales are Scotland's last surviving heavy horses.

Below: The Ardennais is a fine-looking carthorse and still used in France, Sweden and Belgium.

Left: This young cob, a Franches Montagnes, has had its mane neatly clipped.

Above: An Ardennais mare with foal. These large but compact horses from the Ardennes region in France have been used on farms since the Middle Ages, but their numbers are declining.

MINIATURE HORSES

Small horses are ideal mounts for children, but some breeds are so tiny that it would not really be practical to ride them at all. These midget horses, or miniatures as they are called, are usually kept for their novelty value or as pets, a possible option for anyone who loves horses but does not have the space to keep a full-size one. They are certainly unusual and attract a lot of attention at shows.

The smallest horse in the world stands less than seven hands high – about 72cm(28in) – and is the result of crossing a tiny Thoroughbred stallion with a Shetland mare. These pretty Falabellas from Argentina make friendly, good-natured little pets.

Other breeds may be small, but they are strong and sturdy and often specially bred as a child's horse. Standing at 12 hands or under, their shape and build really class them as miniature horses, rather than ponies, although the distinction is not clearly defined. The versatile Pony of the Americas, for example, looks more like a miniature Quarter Horse – a well-proportioned American breed, recognized as probably the most popular in the world. The Chincoteague and Assateague, named after two islands off the southeastern coast of the USA, also look more like small, sturdy horses than ponies. The fine-boned

Caspian is an attractive, yet hardy, miniature horse with an Arablike look to the head. The nimble Indonesian Timor is only 11 hands high and popular with children, but is strong enough to carry a fully grown man all day. Another popular breed measuring less than 12 hands, and a favourite with children, is the Welsh Mountain pony. It has a short, muscular body and intelligent nature.

Left: These two friends clearly illustrate the tremendous variation in size between a large horse and a miniature one; one is a mammoth 17 hands high, the other a mere 80cm(32in).

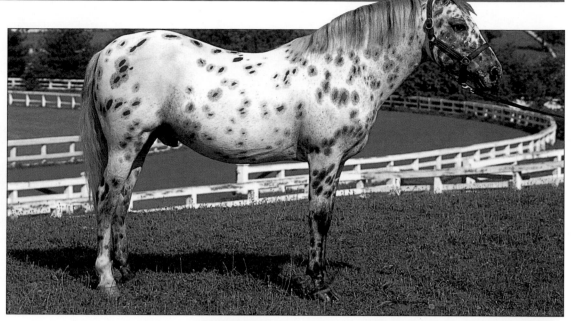

Above: Some horses, although they are quite small, can be very strong for their size. They often have surprising staying power, being capable of pulling a trap at a brisk trot, as well as at a walking pace. Here, the trap is coupled up to the horse with a harness that leaves it just enough leg room to move.

Right: The Falabella is the smallest horse in the world, little bigger than a large dog. It is named after the family that first bred it on a ranch near Buenos Aires in Argentina 100 years ago. These pretty animals are so small that they cannot be ridden, even by children, but are bred as a hobby and kept as pets.

Left: Miniature horses have a charm and attraction all of their own and some examples are kept in zoos throughout the world to safeguard them against extinction or just for their own safety. This brown dwarf pony and grey Pygmy horse are kept in a Frankfurt zoo, away from danger and out of harm of other animals - especially man. The only advantage of keeping these animals in captivity is to monitor their breeding and to allow people to go and see them in the flesh without having to travel to some remote region.

Above: The popular Pony of the Americas was bred in the 1950s in Iowa. It was produced by crossing a Shetland pony stallion with an Appaloosa mare, and a strikingly coloured quality miniature colt was the result.

Right: Miniature horses and ponies come in a variety of different colours, as illustrated here. They are ideal as the first choice of horse for children who want to learn to ride.

PONIES FOR RIDING AND WORK

Any horse measuring less than 14.2 hands can be classed as a pony, and this wide and varied selection of breeds is much in demand for riding schools and as a children's pet. A good riding pony should be gentle-natured and sturdy, with plenty of stamina.

The Shetland pony native to the Scottish Isles, is probably the best-loved and most suited to all these requirements. It is a tiny, yet extremely strong horse, measuring between 65cm(26in) and 105cm(42in) high. The American Shetland is slightly taller but, like its ancestor, is excellent for riding and driving.

Some ponies are also suited to adult riders. Their sure-footedness, hardiness and stamina make them useful mounts across difficult terrain. For example, you can ride an Iceland pony for a considerable distance before it becomes tired, and the lean Mediterranean Balearic makes a patient and useful pony for farmers.

Compact and sturdy, with a patient and obedient nature, ponies have also worked for people for centuries. Easily managed, yet strong and hardy, many of them survive a considerable amount of neglect. Their strength and manageability have made them suitable for farming and industrial tasks, and a useful beast of burden, as well as good for general riding and driving duties.

Often, a pony breed will have been developed to suit a particular task. In Yugoslavia, breeding of the compact and hardy Bosnian is strictly controlled, with some 500,000 of them at work as farm and pack ponies. Mountain farmers still value the Norwegian Fiord pony, whose hardiness and flexibility are more appropriate than any motor vehicle.

The Russians bred the Viatka for a very different purpose: hardy and quick on its feet, it used to pull the traditional sledge, or troika, in the USSR. Today, it is used as a good all-purpose pony.

Left: The Welsh pony is an excellent show pony that looks almost like a small hunter. Its pedigree includes thoroughbred blood from a stallion called Merlin. It is strong and active.

Above: Sure-footed and strong, the Indian Spiti is invaluable as a pack pony in the Himalayan Mountains. It is a stocky animal, with plenty of stamina, but can display a grumpy temperament.

Left: The lovable Shetland pony is an ideal mount for young children, but it needs careful training, as it is a strong and intelligent animal.

Below: Some riders take their hobbies seriously, as well as getting pleasure out of riding. The best thing on show day is to take first prize.

Below: A smart turnout for both pony and rider can make the vital difference between success and failure in many competitive events. Valuable points are sometimes deducted by the judging panel if they consider that appearance is not up to the required standard.

Below: Dartmoor ponies have run wild on this English moor at least since the eleventh century. Once used for tin mining and farmwork, they are now an ideal first horse for children.

Above: The Fiord pony was once popular with the Vikings and still looks very much as it must have done then, with the upright mane and striped legs of primeval breeds. It is strong and hardy, and has an even temperament. It is still used as a work pony on the mountain farms of Norway, where it remains the best practical alternative to any motor vehicle.

PERFORMING HORSES

For many centuries, the horse's natural agility, graceful appearance and inbred intelligence have made it a popular subject for training to perform and entertain.

The display might take the form of a simple dressage, where the horse displays the natural movement of a finely proportioned animal. Some trainers teach a troupe of horses to dance to music, to take part in trick-riding at the circus, to kneel, trot around a narrow barrier, or rear up on their hind legs on command. Other traditional displays might involve riding and horse-mounted skills: military displays, Arab riders leaping through hoops of fire, or archery competitions from horseback are just a few examples.

In America, cowboy spectaculars, including not only calf-roping and rodeo-riding, but also steer-wrestling and barrel-racing, test all of a rider's skills. In Africa, elaborately dressed warriors regularly participate in fantasy displays, following a series of symbolic actions. Often, breeders have specially developed a particular type of horse to suit some performing skill.

The spotted Knabstrup is the favoured horse for circus bareback riding, and the brave and nimble Lusitano is the perfect horse for the Portuguese bullfighting ring. The highly intelligent Lippizaner is probably the most famous of all the performing horses. After about seven years of training, this large white horse from the Spanish Riding School of Vienna is able to perform a complicated sequence of medieval war manoeuvres, such as kicks, crouches and rears.

Above: Bullfighting is a dangerous and bloodthirsty exhibition that puts both horse and rider at considerable risk. Horses have to be rigorously trained and are exercised very hard in a restricted space.

Right: The Spanish Riding School in Vienna, founded by the Austrian Imperial Court, is famous for its expertly disciplined Lippizaners. They are taught to jump, kick and trot on the spot in set movements.

Right: The pretty circus pony will change pace, kneel down or rear up on its hindlegs to order at the gentle touch of a special baton.

Left: In the USA, barrel racing is an exciting display of a horse's skill and balance, as well as a stiff test of its speed.

Above: The famous Hungarian Post involves standing with one foot on each of two horses that are galloping in unison.

Below: Andalusians, a highly bred mixture of Barb and Arab blood, are handsome and popular performing horses.

WORKING HORSEPOWER

Long before the age of the tractor, tram and engine, man throughout the world depended on the speed, size and sheer strength of the horse. Even today, in many countries and areas of industry, this adaptable beast is the best and most economical choice for getting the job done efficiently. Among the world's remotest mountain regions, in the Himalayas and Andes, for example, pack horse and mule are the only way to reach isolated villages with essential goods. In London, beer is still delivered by dray horse because it is cheaper than using motor vehicles. Similarly, some areas of France and North America still use these mighty animals on the farm by choice. For all its size and weight, the draft horse, measuring 18 hands high and over, ploughs a neat and tidy furrow, turning quickly in response to the slightest command in a unique form of trust and coordination between horse and master.

Horses are returning to forestry too. Their strength for pulling and loading fallen trees is unmatched, and they can travel over rough ground and into awkward areas far more easily than any tractor. Yet not all working horses are chosen for strength and size. Pit ponies are tiny, bred to pass through narrow passageways to extract the world's copper, lead, tin, slate and coal. The Texan cowboy chooses his horse for speed, spirit and intelligence, and knows nothing can match it for turning a head of cattle or catching a steer.

The pretty harness horse and pony is still popular for pulling carts, traps and carriages in rural areas in most countries: purely for pleasure perhaps in some countries, but for practical preference among America's Amish communities and through necessity in less developed parts of the world. Fine horses used to make up an important part of any country's military strength, their role now reduced to parades and special displays. However, they still play a very important part in civil defence as royal guards and as police horses, for traffic control and special duties.

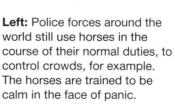

Left: Police forces around the world still use horses in the course of their normal duties, to control crowds, for example. The horses are trained to be calm in the face of panic.

Right: In Switzerland, the military use horses for carrying vital supplies and equipment across the mountains and hills, often in the snow, when it is impossible to take modern machinery and transport.

Left: The larger, heavier horses are often the main attraction at shows, where their sheer size and beauty draw the crowds.

Above: In India, the Rajkot Police select the finest breeds for their purposes and employ them for a variety of tasks.

Above: Although not such a familiar sight today, the farmers in years gone by depended heavily on their faithful horses.

Right: For many years, the stockman (or cowhand) has relied on his horse to approach close to the roaming cattle. From the saddle, he can catch or inspect the animals with the minimum of disturbance.

Left: Important buildings in Spain are regularly guarded by patrols of special mounted guards on Andalusians. In other countries, horses are a common sight on ceremonial occasions.

Below: These Belgian heavy draft horses are strong and intelligent, capable of working together as a team, and completely in the command of the drover that steers them.

Above: Horse-drawn toboggans are a popular and traditional form of transport in Switzerland.

WILD HORSES

Sadly, as time goes by, the number of truly wild horses around the world is diminishing – partly due to domestication or hunting, and partly because their habitat is forever shrinking, even though many of these remarkable animals are hardy and adaptable enough to survive the hottest and most inhospitable terrain or the coldest mountain regions.

The Brumby is a typical example of such a horse; very few remain today, largely because they were considered an agricultural nuisance in their native Australia. The tough Mustang that once thronged America's plainlands has suffered a similar fate; they were shot in vast numbers because of the damage they did to pastureland, and because they were a cheap form of meat. Few survive today, apart from the 'bucking Broncos' used in rodeo shows. The 40 or 50 herds of wild horses surviving on Sable Island off the coast of Nova Scotia somehow withstand the most extreme winters on a diet of little more than rough grass. The tough, rangy wild ponies that live in the mountains of Skyros, a Greek island, endure scorching summer heat and severe cold in the winter.

Some breeds of wild or semi-wild horse closely resemble their ancient forbears. Przewalski's horse, or the Mongolian wild horse, is one of the three primeval types from which all horses and ponies are descended. It survives in zoos and in an ever-diminishing and barren habitat in the mountains on the western edge of the Gobi Desert. Thought to be little changed since the Ice Age, the horse has a short, rough, upright mane, a large heavy head on a short neck and a dark stripe along the back.

Above: The beautiful wild horses of the Camargue live in Southern France, in the watery Rhone delta. Every year, some stock is selected for training.

Left: Today, the wild western Mustangs, or 'Broncos', from the American great plains are virtually extinct. They were traditionally ridden in rodeos.

Right: The wild Exmoor ponies are said to be the oldest native breeds of horse in the UK. Their habitat is in the moorlands of southwest England. They measure between 11 and 12.3 hands, but are strong and have been used as pack animals.

Left: A few herds of wild horses still exist today. One of these is Przewalski's horse from western Mongolia, a hardy breed, forced to live off harsh barren land because man has taken up most of the better grazing grounds. In the past, they were hunted for meat, but are now protected.

Right: Clearly, wild horses are just as likely to fall ill or get injured as domesticated breeds. Fortunately, refuges like this one have been set up to take care of them until they are fit again.

Right: The wild, but privately owned, Dülmen ponies are rounded up for the annual catching of the young colts.

Below: The Spanish Mustang, a relative of the American Mustang, is a light-framed and hardy type of horse.

INDEX

Page numbers in **bold** indicate major references, including accompanying photographs. Page numbers in *italics* indicate captions to other illustrations. Less important text entries are shown in normal type.

PICTURE CREDITS

Photographers
The publishers wish to thank the following photographers and
agencies who have supplied photographs for this book. The
photographers have been credited by page number and position on
the page: (B) Bottom, (T) Top, (C) Centre, (BL) Bottom Left, etc.

Bob Langrish: 9(BR), 10(B), 11(T,C), 12, 12-13(CB), 13(TL,CR),
14-15(BC), 15(TR,BR), 16(CR,BR), 17(BR), 18(BL), 18-19(BC), 19(TL),
20(T,BL), 21(TR,C,BL), 22(T,BL), 24(TC,BR), 25(TC,TR,C,BR), 26(T),
27(T,C,CR), 28, 29(T,CL,BL), 35(TL,TR,BR), 36(B), 37(CL),
41(C,BR), 42(BL), 43(C), 44(T,BL), 45(BR), 46(BL), 47(T), 48-9(TC),
48(BR), 49(C), 51, 52(T,BL), 53(T), 54(T,BR), 56(T,BL), 58(BL)

Photo Researchers Inc.:
Linda Bartlett: 37(BL)
Rainer Berg/Okapia: 32(BL), 33(T), 35(CL)
Arthus-Bertrand/Jacana: 16(T)
Labat-Y.A. Bertrand/Jacana: 57(BL)
Gabriele Boiselle/Okapia: 10(T), 26(B), 33(BR), 39(BR), 57(CR)
C. J. Collins: 23(TL), 37(BR)
Jerry Cooke: 34(BL), 40(BC)
Gerry Cranham: 30(T), 47(BR), 57(CB)
Ray Ellis: 32(BR), 44-5(BC)
Victor Englebert 19(TR)
David R. Frazier: 17(CR)
Geoff Gilbert/Southern Living: 21(TL)
Guy Gillette: 57(TR)
Francois Gohier: 53(CL)
Farrell Grehan 9(TR,CL)
Christian Grzimek/Okapia: 8(T)
Tom Hollyman: 27(B)
George Holton: 9(BL)
Richard Hutchings: 17(CL), 22(BC), 55(TR)
Dana Hyde 37(TR)
Susan Johns: 23(C)
J. Klein/Okapia: 34(BR), 35(BL)

Paolo Koch: 37(TL)
Renee Lynn: 36(T)
Robert Maier/Okapia: 38-9(TC), 39(TR), 53(BR), 59(B)
Helen Marcus: 16(BL)
Francis Mayer 8(BR)
Lawrence Migdale 37(CR)
William Munoz: 31(BL), 59(TR,CL)
Tom McHugh: Contents page 4(B), 6(BL,BR) 7(T,BR), 9(BL), 31(TR),
50(BR), 58-9(TC)
Joseph Nettis: 20(BR)
R. van Nostrand: 50(BL)
Okapia: 42(BR), 47(BL), 50-1(TC)
Walter D. Osborne 49(TR)
Stan Pantovic: 24(BL)
Carl Purcell: 17(TR)
Fritz Prenzell/Okapia: Title page, 43(BR)
Bonnie Rauch: 23(BR)
Hans Reinhard/Okapia: 14(BL), 17(BL), 31(TL), 33(BL), 55(B)
Kjell B. Sandved: 43(TL)
H. W. Silvester/Rapho: 58(C)
St. Meyers/Okapia 22-3(BC)
Southern Living: 46(T)
Art Stein: 15(CL)
Jean-Philippe Varin/Jacana: 7(BL)
Elisabeth Weiland: Contents page 4-5(T), 9(TL), 11(B), 13(TR,BR)
14-15(TC), 18(TR), 19(CL,BR), 21(BR), 23(TR), 25(CB), 29(BR), 30,
31(BR), 33(CL), 34(T,CR), 38(B), 39(C,BL), 40(T,BL), 40-1(BC), 41(T),
42(T), 43(TR,BL), 45(TL,TR,C), 46(BR), 48(BL,C), 49(BL,BR), 52(BR),
54(BL), 55(TL), 56(BR), 57(B), 59(CR)
Larry West: 32(T)
Jeanne White: 6(T)